MATH ADVENTURES

Digging
for
Dinosaurs

by Wendy Clemson
and David Clemson

Math and curriculum consultant:
Debra Voege, M.A.,
science and math curriculum
resource teacher

GARETH**STEVENS**
GS
P U B L I S H I N G
A Member of the WRC Media Family of Companies

Please visit our web site at:
www.garethstevens.com
For a free color catalog describing Gareth Stevens Publishing's list of high-quality books and multimedia programs, call 1-800-542-2595 (USA) or 1-800-387-3178 (Canada). Gareth Stevens Publishing's fax: (414) 332-3567

Library of Congress Cataloging-in-Publication Data

Clemson, Wendy.
  Digging for dinosaurs / Wendy Clemson and David Clemson. — North American ed.
     p. cm. — (Math adventures)
   ISBN-13: 978-0-8368-7838-7 (lib. bdg.)
   ISBN-13: 978-0-8368-8137-0 (softcover)
   1. Mathematics—Problems, exercises, etc.—Juvenile literature.
   2. Paleontology—Juvenile literature. 3. Dinosaurs—Juvenile literature.
   I. Clemson, David. II. Title.
   QA43.C6555   2006
   510—dc22   2006052245

This North American edition first published in 2007 by
Gareth Stevens Publishing
A Member of the WRC Media Family of Companies
330 West Olive Street, Suite 100
Milwaukee, WI 53212 USA

This U.S. edition copyright © 2007 by Gareth Stevens, Inc. Original edition copyright © 2007 by ticktock Entertainment Ltd. First published in Great Britain in 2006 by ticktock Media Ltd., Unit 2, Orchard Business Centre, North Farm Road, Tunbridge Wells, Kent, TN2 3XF.

ticktock project editor: Rebecca Clunes
ticktock project designer: Sara Greasley
Gareth Stevens editor: Tea Benduhn
Gareth Stevens art direction: Tammy West
Gareth Stevens graphic designer: Kami Strunsee
Gareth Stevens production: Jessica Yanke and Robert Kraus

Picture credits
t=top, b=bottom, c=center, l=left, r=right, fl=far left, fr=far right
Lisa Alderson 1, 2, 26b, 27t, 31t; BananaStock/Alamy 4br; David R. Frazier Photolibrary, Inc./Alamy 14t; Roger Harris/Science Photo Library 27b; Simon Mendez 6l, 6r, 17, 14bl, 14bfr, 14br, 24t, 26t, 29b, 31b, 32; Larry Miller/Science Photo Library 18; The Natural History Museum, London 24b, 25; Louie Psihoyos/Corbis 19; Luis Rey 5, 6c, 7b, 8l, 11b, 21, 23, 29t, 30; Royalty-Free/Corbis 15t; Shutterstock 4tl, 4bl, 4tr, 8-9, 9t, 15b, 20, 27cl, 27c, 28t, 28bl; Sinclair Stammers/Science Photo Library 13; Ticktock Media Archive 7t, 10, 11t, 12t, 12b, 14bfl, 27cr, 28bfl, 28br, 28bfr.

Printed in Canada

1 2 3 4 5 6 7 8 9 10 10 09 08 07 06

CONTENTS

MEASUREMENT CONVERSIONS

1 inch = 2.5 centimeters
1 foot = 0.3 meter
1 ounce = 28.3 grams
1 pound = 0.5 kilogram

1 ton = 0.9 tonne
1 cup = 240 milliliters
1 pint = 0.5 liter
1 gallon = 3.8 liters

LET'S START DIGGING

You have an exciting job. You are a dinosaur expert! You try to find dinosaur bones, eggs, and footprints. Fossils help you learn about the ways dinosaurs lived millions of years ago, then you tell everybody else what you have learned!

Digging for dinosaur bones, eggs, and footprints is an exciting and important job.

Dinosaur experts look for bones that have been buried for millions of years.

Dinosaur experts write about their finds and read what other scientists have written.

Museums display the dinosaur discoveries the experts find.

Sometimes, dinosaur experts talk to children about their jobs.

Did you know that dinosaur experts need to use math?

Inside this book, you will find math puzzles that dinosaur experts have to solve every day. You will also have a chance to answer number questions about bones and fossils.

What is inside the book?

Find out what needs to be done in your busy day.

Charts and tables will help you answer the math questions.

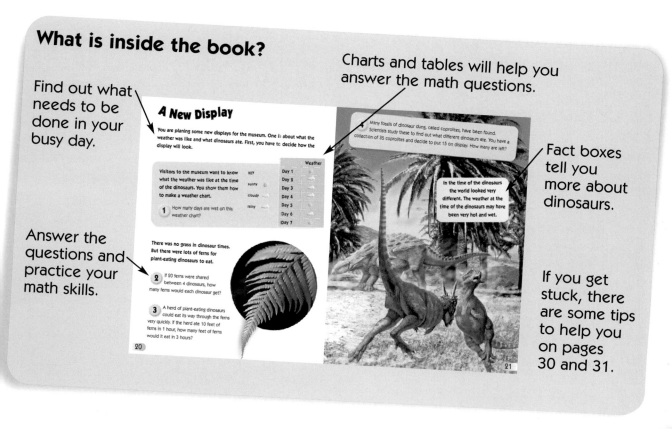

A New Display

You are planing some new displays for the museum. One is about what the weather was like and what dinosaurs ate. First, you have to decide how the display will look.

Visitors to the museum want to know what the weather was like at the time of the dinosaurs. You show them how to make a weather chart.

1. How many days are wet on this weather chart?

There was no grass in dinosaur times. But there were lots of ferns for plant-eating dinosaurs to eat.

2. If 20 ferns were shared between 4 dinosaurs, how many ferns would each dinosaur get?

3. A herd of plant-eating dinosaurs could eat its way through the ferns very quickly. If the herd ate 10 feet of ferns in 1 hour, how many feet of ferns would it eat in 3 hours?

20

Many fossils of dinosaur dung, called coprolites, have been found. Scientists study these to find out what different dinosaurs ate. You have a collection of 35 coprolites and decide to put 15 on display. How many are left?

In the time of the dinosaurs the world looked very different. The weather at the time of the dinosaurs may have been very hot and wet.

21

Fact boxes tell you more about dinosaurs.

Answer the questions and practice your math skills.

If you get stuck, there are some tips to help you on pages 30 and 31.

Are you ready to be a dinosaur expert for the day?

You will need paper, a pencil, and a ruler, and don't forget to bring your shovel. Let's go!

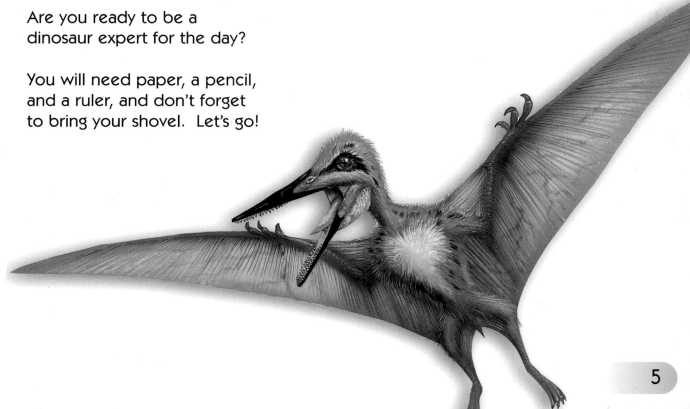

WALKING WITH DINOSAURS

Looking for dinosaurs is not as difficult as you might think. Dinosaurs roamed Earth for millions of years, and they left a lot of signs behind, including bones, eggs, and footprints. Today, you are going to search for dinosaur bones in the United States and Canada.

Dinosaurs lived during three different periods of time.

- Cretaceous period

- Jurassic period

- Triassic period

The map to the right shows some sites where dinosaur fossils have been found.

Map of the United States and Canada

1 How many sites have fossils from the Triassic period?

2 Which period has the most sites?

The dinosaurs below lived during different periods.

Diplodocus
lived 150 million years ago.

Liliensternus
lived 220 million years ago.

Triceratops
lived 70 million years ago.

3 Which dinosaur lived longest ago?

You arrive at a site in the desert, where the ground is dry and rocky. You know that dinosaurs used to live here. Suddenly, you see a giant footprint.

4 Look at the picture to the right, which shows a hand next to a dinosaur's footprint. How many hands do you think might fit inside the footprint?

A 1 hand   **B** 4 hands   **C** 14 hands

Some dinosaurs lived in groups called herds. Staying in a group helped protect the dinosaurs from enemies. Some herds may have been very large. Dinosaur experts have found up to 30 dinosaur skeletons in one place.

5 You can make 30 by adding the same number many times. 30 is the same as 30 ones. 30 is also the same as 3 tens. How many twos make 30?

Amargasaurus may have traveled in herds. This dinosaur was 30 feet long and had two rows of spines down its neck.

WHOSE FOOTPRINT?

You find a dinosaur footprint and want to know which dinosaur left it. You look through a book to find a picture of the footprint. The footprint you found looks like the footprint of *Iguanodon*. This dinosaur usually walked on all four feet. It could also stand on just its back feet, which made *Iguanodon* different from other dinosaurs.

This dinosaur footprint shows 3 toes of a dinosaur's back foot.

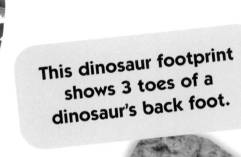

1 The footprint you found is from one of *Iguanodon*'s back feet. It shows 3 toes. *Iguanodon* had 5 toes on each of its front feet. How many toes did *Iguanodon* have in total?

2 *Iguanodon* was 33 feet long from the tip of its nose to the end of its tail. If its tail was 10 feet long, how long was the rest of *Iguanodon*?

You find 3 more footprints, and you decide to make some plaster casts to take back to the museum.

Plaster Cast Instructions
1. Mix the plaster with some water. Use 2 pints of water for 1 package of plaster.
2. Pour the mixture into the footprint.
3. Wait 5 minutes for the plaster to dry.
4. Carefully lift the plaster cast out of the footprint.

3 It takes you 15 minutes to make each plaster cast. What fraction of these 15 minutes do you spend waiting for the plaster to dry?

    A ½   **B** ¼   **C** ⅓

4 How many pints of water do you need if you use 3 packages of plaster?

5 If you make 8 plaster casts of each of *Iguanodon*'s front feet and 3 plaster casts of each of its back feet, how many plaster casts will you make in total?

6 You draw a plan to show where you found each footprint. Starting from the back left footprint, which footprint did you find 2 squares up and 2 squares right?

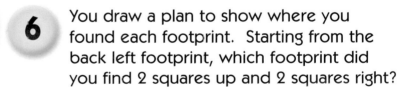

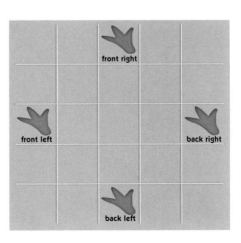

BONY CLUES

You find and collect some small pieces of bones. Then you see something big poking up from the sand. You hurry toward it, careful not to step on any other fossils. The object looks like it might be part of a leg bone from the dinosaur *Stegosaurus*.

Stegosaurus was 30 feet long. It had two lines of plates along its back. At the end of its tail, it had four long, sharp spikes. *Stegosaurus* would swing its spiked tail at attackers.

1 You find a piece of bone that is 20 inches long. If the piece is 1/2 the length of the entire bone, how long was the entire bone?

LENGTH OF BONES

You collect 3 dinosaur bones. You draw a sketch of each bone and write the bone's length under each sketch.

front leg bone
3 feet

hip bone
94 inches

back leg bone
9 inches

2 Put the bones in order from longest to shortest.

You find a tooth! Dinosaur experts can figure out the types of foods dinosaurs ate by the shapes of their teeth. Plant-eaters had teeth that were flat and not very sharp. Meat-eaters had very sharp, pointed teeth.

3 Measure this dinosaur tooth with a ruler. What is its length?

You have a chart that tells you which kinds of dinosaurs ate meat and which kinds of dinosaurs ate plants.

4 How many kinds of dinosaurs on the chart to the right are plant-eaters?

5 How many kinds of dinosaurs are on the chart in total?

plant-eaters	meat-eaters
Diplodocus	Tyrannosaurus
Stegosaurus	Oviraptor
Triceratops	Velociraptor
Iguanodon	

Tyrannosaurus weighed 5 tons. That is more than the weight of 200 children!

FOSSIL FINDS

Next, you visit some cliffs to look for fossils of sea creatures. You are looking for ammonites, which were alive at the time of the dinosaurs. You are also looking for trilobites, which lived millions of years before dinosaurs.

There were more than 10,000 different types of trilobites. Trilobites varied in size from 1 inch to 18 inches.

1 Which of the measurements below is not equal to 18 inches?

    A 1½ feet

    B 1 foot and 6 inches

    C eighteen inches

    D one foot and five inches

    E one and a half feet

Trilobites were among the first living creatures.

2 You find 3 ammonite fossils that look like the one to the left. Each fossil is 5 inches across. You pack them side by side in a box. How wide does the box have to be?

3 You pack another box. This box has 3 rows of fossils with 4 fossils in each row. How many fossils are in the box?

4 Look at the rock above. You can see lots of ammonite fossils. Answer these puzzles.

    A Are the ammonites congruent or similar?

    B Look at the largest ammonite. Use your finger to trace the spiral from the inside to the outside of the ammonite. Does the shape spiral clockwise or counterclockwise?

    C Do ammonites have a line of symmetry?

COUNTING YOUR FINDS

5 You find 4 plant fossils, 9 ammonites, and 6 trilobites. You make a bar graph to show the numbers of the fossils you have found. You look at the bar graph and find a mistake. What is the mistake?

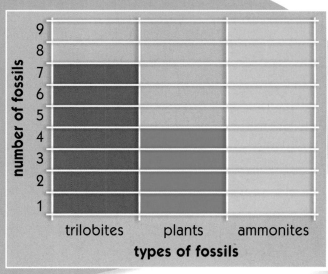

TO THE MUSEUM

You are now going to take your fossils back to the museum.
A helicopter picks you up and flies you to the museum.

The first thing you see at the museum is the skeleton of the mighty *Tyrannosaurus*. When this dinosaur was alive, it walked on its hind legs. It had between 50 and 60 teeth, and it could easily crush the bones of other dinosaurs.

1 Which of these numbers are between 50 and 60?

53   62   75

57   65   49

Tyrannosaurus had a huge head. Its skull was 5 feet long.

Tyrannosaurus was big, but it was not the heaviest dinosaur.
Many plant-eating dinosaurs weighed much more than *Tyrannosaurus*.

Apatosaurus
30 to 38 tons

Triceratops
6 to 12 tons

Tyrannosaurus
5 to 7 tons

Brachiosaurus
33 to 48 tons

2 Look at the greatest weight for each kind of dinosaur shown above. Put the dinosaurs in order from lightest to heaviest.

One of your favorite exhibits at the museum is *Apatosaurus*. This dinosaur usually grew for about 10 years before it was fully grown. It may have lived for 100 years in total.

3 How many tens are in 100?

Apatosaurus had a long neck. It could easily reach the tops of trees to eat.

Triceratops was a plant-eater. Its name means "three-horned face." Its 3 horns helped it defend itself against meat-eaters like *Tyrannosaurus*.

4 There are 5 *Triceratops* on display, how many horns do they have in total?

Triceratops lived in North America. It ate bushes and trees.

You take your dinosaur finds to the museum workroom. You label each bone, tooth, fossil, and footprint. Each label has a special code on it. You put the label codes in three rows, with each row following a pattern.

row A	A2	A4		A8
row B	B3		B9	B12
row C	C10	C15	C20	

1 Choose the correct label codes below to fill in the blank spaces in the rows above.

A1	C26	B8	B6	A6	C25

You also have to measure each of your finds.
Some of the measuring tools you use are shown below.

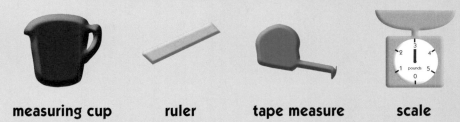

measuring cup   ruler   tape measure   scale

2 Which tool would you use to measure
   A   the length of a bone about the size of your hand?
   B   the weight of a fossil?
   C   the length of a hole dug to find fossils?
   D   water for making a plaster cast?

Stegosaurus might have used its plates to keep warm. The Sun shining on the plates could have heated them up.

You are putting together a model of *Stegosaurus* for display. You have labeled and numbered each of the plates that go on the model's back. The odd-numbered plates will be in one row and the even-numbered plates will be in another row.

3 Sort the plates below into an odd row and an even row.

7 3 10 2 9 8 1 6 13 11 5 4 12 14

DINOSAUR TRACKS

You unpack the plaster casts you made of the dinosaur footprints. You can use the plaster casts to find out more about the dinosaur that made the tracks. You want to figure out the dinosaur's height and how fast it was moving.

1 Using a dinosaur's footprint, you can figure out its height up to its hips. The footprints you found are each 2 feet long. To find out the dinosaur's height up to its hips, you multiply the length of one footprint by 4. How high is your dinosaur up to its hips?

2 The distance a dinosaur travels in 2 steps is called the dinosaur's "stride length." Your dinosaur travels 4 feet in 1 step. What is its stride length?

Using the dinosaur's hip height and stride length, you can figure out how fast it was moving.

3 Divide the dinosaur's stride length by its hip height. What number do you get?

Look at the chart to the right to find where the number fits.

4 Was your dinosaur walking, trotting, or running?

DINOSAUR SPEED

	stride length divided by hip height
walking	less than 2
trotting	between 2 and 3
running	more than 3

Now you want to see if you can make a whole skeleton out of the bone fossils you found.

5 Put the bones below in order, from the head of the dinosaur to its tail.

rib bones   neck bone   front leg bones

skull bones   tail bone

Experts use dinosaur tracks to learn about behavior. One set of tracks means the dinosaur traveled alone. Dinosaurs that traveled in groups left sets of tracks that were side by side.

A NEW DISPLAY

You are planning some new displays for the museum. One display will show the weather during the time of the dinosaurs. Another will show the foods the dinosaurs ate. First, you have to decide what facts to include in your display.

	weather
day 1	☀
day 2	🌧
day 3	☁
day 4	🌧
day 5	☀
day 6	☁
day 7	☀

Visitors to the museum want to know what the weather was like during the time of the dinosaurs. You made the chart to the right, which shows the weather during dinosaur times.

KEY

☀ = sunny

☁ = cloudy

🌧 = rainy

1 How many days are rainy on the weather chart?

During dinosaur times, there were lots of ferns for plant-eating dinosaurs to eat.

2 If 4 dinosaurs shared 20 ferns, how many ferns could each dinosaur eat?

3 A herd of plant-eating dinosaurs could eat its way through ferns very quickly. If the herd ate 10 feet of ferns in 1 hour, how many feet of ferns would the herd eat in 3 hours?

4 Your team of dinosaur experts has found many fossils of dinosaur dung, called coprolites. Scientists study coprolites to find out what foods different dinosaurs ate. You have a collection of 35 coprolites and will put 15 of them on display. How many coprolites from your collection will not be on display?

In the time of the dinosaurs, the world looked very different. The weather at the time of the dinosaurs may have been very hot.

FLYING VISIT

You like studying the creatures that could fly. *Archaeopteryx* is the oldest known bird. It did not fly very well, but it was a fierce hunter.

The chart below shows the measurements of *Archaeopteryx*.

ARCHAEOPTERYX	
length	12 inches
wingspan	20 inches

1 What is the difference between *Archaeopteryx*'s length and wingspan?

2 *Archaeopteryx* had 3 claws on each wing. It used its claws to grasp branches. How many wing claws did it have in total?

3 *Archaeopteryx* ate small animals and insects. How many insects are shown here?

4 *Archaeopteryx* weighed between 10 and 17 ounces. If you put *Archaeopteryx* on a scale, which of the scales below shows the weight of an *Archaeopteryx*?

A

B

During dinosaur times, some reptiles could fly. These flying reptiles, called *pterosaurs*, had wings, but they did not have feathers.

5 If the *pterosaur* to the right makes a quarter turn clockwise, which of the pictures below shows its new position?

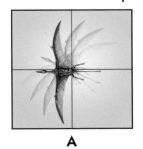

A

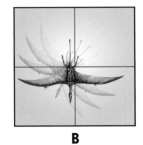

B

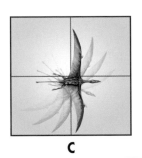

C

6 Your best fossil is going on display. It is a fossil of *Pterodactylus*. This flying reptile was 36 inches long, and it had a wingspan of 6 feet. Which of the labels below is the correct label for the display?

PTERODACTYLUS
Habitat: rivers and seas
Wingspan: 4 feet
Length: 36 inches

label A

PTERODACTYLUS
Habitat: rivers and seas
Wingspan: 6 feet
Length: 36 inches

label B

PTERODACTYLUS
Habitat: rivers and seas
Wingspan: 4 feet
Length: 20 inches

label C

DINOSAUR PARENTS

Like birds and lizards, dinosaurs laid eggs. You decide to make a display that shows a dinosaur nest with eggs in it.

The *Hypselosaurus* laid its eggs in a line as it walked. The eggs below are not in the correct order. You put the eggs in order and see that one is missing.

1 What is the number of the missing egg?

2   8   12   4   6   10   9   13   1   3   7   5

Some dinosaur eggs were very big! The eggs of *Hypselosaurus* were bigger than footballs. They were at least 12 inches across!

2 If you filled a *Hypselosaurus* egg with water, it would hold about 1/2 gallon. How many cups is that?

Maiasaura lived in groups. A group stayed near the eggs that were laid until the babies hatched. Each mother laid between 15 and 20 eggs.

3 Which of these numbers are between 15 and 20?

17   12   25   52
      10   16   19

Just like birds today, *Oviraptors* made nests and sat on their eggs to keep them warm.

4 Look at the hatched dinosaur eggs below. Find the pieces that fit together to make whole eggs.

A B C D

E F G H

Oviraptor was about 6 feet long and walked on two legs.

IS THIS A RECORD?

You have been asked to make a list of dinosaur record breakers. New dinosaur fossils are being found all the time, so records have to be kept up to date.

LONGEST
The longest dinosaurs ate plants. They were so big that they moved very slowly. *Seismosaurus* was among the longest of the plant-eaters.

1 *Seismosaurus* was 110 feet long.
Do you think that is nearest the length of
   A a jump rope?   **B** a bus?   **C** a basketball court?

2 Meat-eating dinosaurs were not as long as plant-eaters. One of the longest meat-eaters was *Tyrannosaurus*. It was 40 feet long. Do you think that is nearest the length of
   A a jump rope?   **B** a bus?   **C** a basketball court?

TALLEST
The tallest dinosaurs, such as *Brachiosaurus*, had long necks. They could reach up to eat the leaves at the tops of tall trees.

3 *Brachiosaurus* was about 85 feet tall. You and your friends stand on each other's shoulders until you are as tall as *Brachiosaurus*. Which number below is closest to the number of people standing on each other's shoulders?

5   **25**   **100**

SMALLEST

One of the smallest dinosaurs was *Bambiraptor*. This dinosaur was only 40 inches long and weighed about 6 pounds.

4 Which of these items might weigh the same as *Bambiraptor*?

egg

shoe

sack of potatoes

Some meat-eating dinosaurs were very small. *Velociraptor* was about 6 feet long — and half of its length was its tail!

IN THE SHOP

All of your displays are now ready for a grand opening. On your way out of the museum, you visit the museum gift shop. You see model insects inside see-through plastic blocks.

The museum has some real insects from dinosaur times. The insects became trapped in a sticky substance called resin, which comes from trees. The resin hardened and turned into amber.

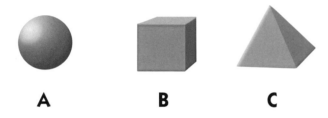

A   B   C

This piece of amber shows insects that were trapped millions of years ago.

1 The museum sells plastic models of amber in the shapes above. What are the names of the shapes?

2 A plastic model costs $1.50. You give the cashier $2.00. How much change will you get?

3 Which of the fossils below is the most expensive?

A   B   C   D

$3.00   75¢ $2.50 $3.75

Brachiosaurus was 40 feet tall, about the height of a four-story building.

4 Look at the poster to the right. How much less is the entrance fee for the grand opening than on a regular day?

5 You bring 2 friends to the grand opening. How much will the entrance fee cost for all of you?

6 You love the exhibition! You go 1 time for the grand opening and 2 times later. How much do you pay in total?

Meet Allosaurus
and other dinosaurs!

Grand Opening
Entrance Fee.................$5
Regular
Entrance Fee................$12

TIPS AND HELP

PAGES 6-7

Longest ago - To find out which dinosaur lived longest ago, put the numbers of years in order. Look at the hundreds first: 150 has one hundred, 220 has two hundreds, and 70 has no hundreds. The number with the most hundreds is the longest ago. In order, the numbers starting from the longest ago are 220 million years ago, then 150 million years ago, and, finally, 70 million years ago.

PAGES 8-9

Subtraction - When you take away the length of *Iguanodon*'s tail from its total body length, you are subtracting.

Fractions - A fraction is part of a whole. When you share, or cut something into 2 equal parts, each part is the fraction ½ (one-half). If you cut something into 3 equal parts, each part is the fraction ⅓ (one-third). If something is cut into 4 equal parts, each part is the fraction ¼ (one-fourth, or one quarter).

PAGES 10-11

Putting measurements in order - Check that the measurements are all in the same unit. Here, you can change all of the measurements to inches. There are 12 inches in 1 foot.

Measuring length - When you use a ruler, place the "0" (zero) at one end of the line you are measuring. To find out the length, read the number on the ruler that is at the other end of the line you are measuring.

PAGES 12-13

Feet and inches - There are 12 inches in 1 foot and 6 inches in ½ foot.

Congruent or similar - Things that are congruent are the same size and shape. Things that are similar are the same shape, but not the same size.

Clockwise - is the direction the hands of a clock move.
Counterclockwise - is the opposite direction.

Line of symmetry - A shape has a line of symmetry if it has 2 halves that match each other exactly when the figure is folded along a line down the center.

PAGES 14-15

Whole numbers between - Think of a number line. Here, the line starts at the number 50 and ends at 60. The number line looks like this:

50	51	52	53	54	55	56	57	58	59	60

Do you see any of the numbers from the math puzzle? Those numbers are your answers.

Groups of three - is the same as counting by threes. The numbers in groups of three are also the products in the three times (3 x) table. To count by threes, count out loud: 3, 6, 9, 12, 15, 18, 21, 24, 27, 30, 33, 36, and so on.

PAGES 16-17

Measuring tools - It is important to choose the right measuring tool for a job. We use a cup to measure liquids, and we use a scale to measure weight. We use a ruler to measure inches, and we use a tape measure to measure feet.

Odds and evens - Even numbers are the numbers in the counting pattern of twos: 2, 4, 6, 8, 10, 12, 14, 16, 18, 20, and so on. Odd numbers are all the numbers that are not even: 1, 3, 5, 7, 9, 11, 13, 15, 17, 19, and so on.

PAGES 18-19

Multiplication - Multiplying is the same as repeated addition. Here, 2 x 4 gives the same answer as 2 four times (2 + 2 + 2 + 2) or 4 two times (4 + 4).

Division - When you divide a number, you split the first number into as many equal parts as the second number is. So, if you divide 8 by 8, you split 8 eight times, which leaves 8 groups of 1.

PAGES 20-21

Sharing - Sharing is the same as dividing. Here, you can find out how many ferns each dinosaur would eat if each dinosaur had the same number of ferns.

PAGES 22-23

Pound - 1 pound is 16 ounces.
A ¼ turn - There are 4 ¼ (one-quarter) turns in 1 complete turn.

PAGES 24-25

Gallon - 1 gallon is 16 cups.

PAGES 26-27

Longest, tallest, smallest - We say "longer," "taller," or "smaller" to compare two things. We say "longest," "tallest," and "smallest" when comparing three or more things.

PAGES 28-29

Dollar - 1 dollar is 100 cents.

ANSWERS

PAGES 6-7

1 6 sites
2 Cretaceous period
3 *Liliensternus*
4 B (4 hands)
5 15 twos

PAGES 8-9

1 16 toes
2 23 feet long
3 ⅓
4 6 pints of water
5 22 plaster casts
6 back right

PAGES 10-11

1 40 inches
2 hip bone
    front leg bone
    back leg bone
3 2½ inches
4 4 dinosaurs
5 7 dinosaurs

PAGES 12-13

1 D (one foot and
    five inches)
2 15 inches wide
3 12 fossils
4 A = similar
    B = clockwise
    C = no
5 the graph shows
    7 trilobites instead
    of 6 trilobites

PAGES 14-15

1 53 and 57
2 *Tyrannosaurus*
    Triceratops
    Apatosaurus
    Brachiosaurus
3 10
4 15 horns

PAGES 16-17

1 row A = A6
    row B = B6
    row C = C25
2 A = ruler
    B = scale
    C = tape measure
    D = measuring cup
3 odd row = 1, 3,
    5, 7, 9, 11, and 13
    even row = 2, 4,
    6, 8, 10, 12, and 14

PAGES 18-19

1 8 feet
2 8 feet
3 1
4 walking
5 skull bones,
    neck bone, front
    leg bones, rib
    bones, tail bone

PAGES 20-21

1 2 days
2 5 ferns
3 30 feet
4 20 coprolites

PAGES 22-23

1 8 inches
2 6 wing claws
3 16 insects
4 B
5 C
6 label B

PAGES 24-25

1 11
2 8 cups
3 16, 17, and 19
4 A and D
    B and E
    C and H
    F and G

PAGES 26-27

1 C (a basketball
    court)
2 B (a bus)
3 25 people
4 sack of
    potatoes

PAGES 28-29

1 A = sphere
    B = cube
    C = pyramid
2 50 cents
3 D ($3.75)
4 $7
5 $15
6 $29